Daily Spanish For Beginners

How To Easily Speak Spanish With Only 12 Minutes Of Practice A Day

By

Celestino Rivas

Table of Contents

Introduction

¡Hola! It's so nice to meet you! My name is Celestino, and I'm going to be the guide in your journey to learning the language of Miguel de Cervantes, Shakira, Isabel Allende, Marc Anthony, and that beauty down the block you've been trying to talk to.

Of course, we're speaking about: *El español!*

Now that you decided to take the time and effort necessary to learn Spanish, the next step is finding a book you can use to learn the very basics of the language, getting some level one vocabulary, helping you understand some grammar, and even giving you some pronunciation tips. You need a book to help you get started in your Spanish learning path in a fun, didactical, and applicable to daily life way.

Got you covered on that: *Daily Spanish* is exactly the book you're looking for!

In these daily lessons, you'll find little pills of knowledge that will take you no more than 10 minutes to learn but will keep you honing your Spanish speaking skills so that you can speak the language in a social context on the shortest amount of time possible.

You'll learn what to say when meeting someone, how to ask for directions, how to tell the time, etc. and will also be able to understand what kind of food that restaurant menu is all about. These are daily life situations you could encounter anytime, where having some knowledge of Spanish comes really handy.

How do I know about this? Well, as a Spanish as a Foreign Language (SFL) teacher with more than 20 years of working experience, I know which words, phrases, and grammatical concepts are the fundamental ones to learn and have taught hundreds of students how to communicate in social situations all around the Spanish speaking world.

We're talking about very basic stuff, not too difficult to learn, that will open the doors for you to having conversations with people from many different backgrounds, making it possible for you to keep on learning Spanish along the way.

What's better to break the ice with someone and start building a friendship than speaking their own language? As some random guy called Nelson Mandela once said:

"If you talk to a man in a language he understands, that goes to his head. If you talk to him in his language, that goes to his heart".

That's what we're talking about here. After reading this book, you'll have a head start and build the momentum to keep learning Spanish every day, just by having day-to-day experiences and meeting people, listening to songs, reading books, and immersing yourself in a rich, multinational and multi-ethnical culture.

This book will be both your cheat sheet and the foundation of your new Spanish-speaking persona. You'll not only learn a language but will take a look at life from a different angle, with a new set of eyes that see the world the way Hispanic people do.

Want to get started? ¡Vamos!

A Note On Pronunciation

One of the things that make Spanish such a beautiful and melodic language it's the special way its words are pronounced: sometimes they seem soft, other times a little tougher, but always flow in an easy and steady manner that is so pleasing to the ears that some very influential people in the past have said things like this:

"I speak Spanish to God, Italian to Women, French to men and German to my horse." Charles V, Holy Roman Emperor

It is indeed very easy to know how to pronounce a word correctly from the way it's written: you only need to know the sound of each letter or group of letters and then combine those sounds in order to produce a word.

Another distinct feature of Spanish is that almost 80% of the words are stressed on the penultimate syllable.

So, if you don't know where to stress the sound of a word (and you'll learn how to find that out later), your safest bet is to always go for the penultimate syllable.

Day 1. The Spanish Vowels

There are only 5 different vocalic sounds in Spanish, and they are way more distinct between one another that they are in English. They're also easier to learn and recognize in a text because most of the time, when you see then in writing, the sound they represent it's always going to be the same.

There are some exceptions, of course, but you'll learn how to distinguish those cases later in the book: there's no need to worry about that now!

Native Spanish speakers can spot a "gringo" from a mile away just by paying attention to the way they pronounce their vowels: English native speakers tend to mix the vowels up, a thing no native Spanish speaker would ever do. It is very important to get this right from the beginning in order to learn the language properly.

The five Spanish vowels are A, E, I, O, U.

They have short, very simple sounds, completely different from one another.

You are familiar with these sounds even though you don't know it yet; just read below, and you'll see how each vowel sounds according to some very common English words:

- The vowel "**A**" sounds like in Apple, Ana, Father, Man, Andy, Chat.
- The vowel "**E**" sounds like in Elegant, Elephant, Elliott, Test, and Text.
- The vowel "**I**" sounds like in Be, See, We, Me, Weed, Feet, Fit, Keep.
- The vowel "**O**" sounds like in October, Organ, Onion, Oregon, and Orlando.
- The vowel "**U**" sounds like in Good, Flute, Foot, Boot, Tune.

Once you get these sounds, internalize them and make them a part of your brain, it will be easier for you to see a Spanish word and associate each vowel to their respective sound.

The key to learning faster:

PRACTICE, PRACTICE, and PRACTICE SOME MORE. Then repeat the process as many times as you wish!

Day 2. Basic Words

When babies are learning to speak, what they do is involving every single one of their senses in the process by paying close attention to what's happening around them.

They SEE things and begin forming concepts in their minds. Then they LISTEN to the way other people call these things and make the connections accordingly.

That's an automatic process. We don't need to worry about it, because children will learn it organically, in a natural process. It's a natural learning system.

We, as adults, can learn that way too. The only thing we need is to focus on that and put our minds to it in order to facilitate the learning process.

So, let's dive in!

What comes next are some very basic words that you can associate with the images shown beside them. Just pay attention to those images, and you'll automatically make the connections to the concepts you have already formed in your mind for them. These words will be very useful in the next lessons to continue learning the language.

Hombre	Man	Lápiz	Pencil
Hombres	Men	Bolígrafo	Pen
Mujer	Woman	Mesa	Table
Mujeres	Women	Silla	Chair
Niño	Boy	Libro	Book
Niña	Girl	Cuaderno	Notebook
Niños	Children	Cocina	Kitchen
Personas	People	Agua	Water
Bebé	Baby	Manzana	Apple
Casa	House	Naranja	Orange
Edificio	Building	Tomate	Tomato
Ventana	Window	Banana	Banana
Puerta	Door	Helado	Ice Cream
Bicicleta	Bicycle	Pan	Bread
Pelota	Ball	Salsa De Tomate	Ketchup
Muñeca	Doll	Arroz	Rice
Árbol	Tree	Blanco	White
Flor	Flower	Negro	Black
Carro	Car	Azul	Blue
Camioneta	Truck	Verde	Green
Perro	Dog	Rojo	Red
		Marrón	Brown

Day 3. Cognates – A Natural Bridge Between Languages

Cognates are words in different languages that share the same etymological origin. This happens because languages are not created in the blink of an eye: they evolve, merge, form, and influence one another through centuries of interaction as the people trade, share knowledge, visit other countries, and yes, even when they fight each other.

English and Spanish are two languages with European origins: one derives from Proto-Germanic and the other from Vulgar Latin. Even before the modern languages got their current form, they've been interacting, and after that, they have been swapping terms and influencing one another for centuries. The result: there are estimates that say that approximately 30 to 40% of all English words have a Spanish cognate. That's an excellent first step to learn the language!

But not all of the cognates are made equal. There are

several types, as explained below:

- **Perfect cognates** are words that are identical in both English and Spanish. These are the easiest to remember and apply in everyday interactions.

- **Near perfect cognates** look very similar in both languages and mean the same things, but require a simple formula to be converted from English to Spanish and vice versa.

- **False cognates**, also known as "false friends", because they are a little two-faced son of... words that, even when spelled in the same or similar manner, have a completely different meaning that can get you in not so nice predicaments. It's better to know who is real, and who is not, right?

It will be very useful to you to memorize the following words in order to leverage the vocabulary advantage of knowing a huge number of Spanish terms even before staring your studies of the language. You can find some common cognates on the lists below.

Day 4. Perfect Cognates

The following words will give you a head start in your Spanish learning quest because they have a perfect equivalent in English that you already know. Taking advantage of them is a must as it can help you build a solid foundation of Spanish vocabulary

Actor	Actor	Chocolate	Chocolate
Admirable	Admirable	Circular	Circular
Agenda	Agenda	Civil	Civil
Alcohol	Alcohol	Club	Club
Altar	Altar	Collar	Collar
Animal	Animal	Colonial	Colonial
Área	Area	Coma	Coma
Artificial	Artificial	Combustión	Combustion
Auto	Auto	Conclusión	Conclusion
Balance	Balance	Conductor	Conductor
Bar	Bar	Confusión	Confusion
Base	Base	Considerable	Considerable
Brutal	Brutal	Control	Control
Cable	Cable	Cordial	Cordial
Canal	Canal	Criminal	Criminal
Cáncer	Cancer	Crisis	Crisis
Canon	Canon	Cultural	Cultural
Capital	Capital	Debate	Debate
Carbón	Carbon	Decisión	Decision
Cartón	Carton	Diagonal	Diagonal
Central	Central	Dimensión	Dimension
Cerebral	Cerebral	Director	Director
Cheque	Cheque	Disco	Disco

División	Division	Inevitable	Inevitable
Doctor	Doctor	Inferior	Inferior
Drama	Drama	Informal	Informal
Editorial	Editorial	Informativa	Informative
Electoral	Electoral	Inseparable	Inseparable
Elemental	Elemental	Inspector	Inspector
Enigma	Enigma	Interminable	Interminable
Error	Error	Invasión	Invasion
Exclusive	Exclusive	Invisible	Invisible
Excursión	Excursion	Irregular	Irregular
Experimental	Experimental	Judicial	Judicial
Explosión	Explosion	Kilo	Kilo
Expulsión	Expulsion	Lateral	Lateral
Extensión	Extension	Legal	Legal
Exterior	Exterior	Liberal	Liberal
Factor	Factor	Literal	Literal
Familiar	Familiar	Local	Local
Fatal	Fatal	Macho	Macho
Federal	Federal	Maestro	Maestro
Festival	Festival	Mango	Mango
Final	Final	Manía	Mania
Flexible	Flexible	Manual	Manual
Formal	Formal	Marginal	Marginal
Formula	Formula	Mate	Mate
Frontal	Frontal	Material	Material
Fundamental	Fundamental	Matrimonial	Matrimonial
Gala	Gala	Medieval	Medieval
Gas	Gas	Mediocre	Mediocre
General	General	Melón	Melon
Génesis	Genesis	Mental	Mental
Global	Global	Menú	Menu
Grave	Grave	Metal	Metal
Habitual	Habitual	Miserable	Miserable
Hobby	Hobby	Moral	Moral
Horizontal	Horizontal	Mortal	Mortal
Horror	Horror	Motel	Motel
Hospital	Hospital	Motor	Motor
Hotel	Hotel	Múltiple	Multiple
Idea	Idea	Municipal	Municipal
Ideal	Ideal	Musical	Musical
Imperial	Imperial	Natural	Natural
Implacable	Implacable	Noble	Noble
Incursión	Incursion	Normal	Normal
Individual	Individual	Nostalgia	Nostalgia
Industrial	Industrial	Ópera	Opera

Oral	Oral	Secular	Secular
Oriental	Oriental	Sentimental	Sentimental
Original	Original	Serial	Serial
Panorama	Panorama	Sexual	Sexual
Particular	Particular	Similar	Similar
Pasta	Pasta	Simple	Simple
Pastor	Pastor	Singular	Singular
Patio	Patio	Social	Social
Patrón	Patron	Solar	Solar
Peculiar	Peculiar	Solo	Solo
Penal	Penal	Subversión	Subversion
Perfume	Perfume	Superficial	Superficial
Personal	Personal	Superior	Superior
Peseta	Peseta	Taxi	Taxi
Piano	Piano	Televisión	Television
Plaza	Plaza	Terrible	Terrible
Plural	Plural	Terror	Terror
Popular	Popular	Total	Total
Pretensión	Pretension	Transcendental	Transcendental
Principal	Principal	Triple	Triple
Probable	Probable	Tropical	Tropical
Propaganda	Propaganda	Unión	Unión
Protector	Protector	Universal	Universal
Provincial	Provincial	Usual	Usual
Radical	Radical	Verbal	Verbal
Radio	Radio	Versión	Version
Región	Region	Vertical	Vertical
Regional	Regional	Violín	Violin
Regular	Regular	Visible	Visible
Religión	Religion	Visual	Visual
Reunión	Reunion	Vital	Vital
Revisión	Revision	Vulgar	Vulgar
Ritual	Ritual	Vulnerable	Vulnerable
Rural	Rural		

A word of caution: remember pronunciation rules are different in Spanish, so it's almost certain that the cognate words will be pronounced differently in both languages. In order to know where to stress words, keep in mind that in Spanish, the vast majority of words are *graves*, or have the stress in the second-to-last syllable and are not accentuated. For the rest of the words, you'll see an accent mark at the top of the vocal where the stress of the word must be.

Day 5. Near Perfect Cognates

The following near perfect cognates follow the rule for nouns ending **'tion'** in English can be converted to Spanish by replacing with a **'ción'**.

Abstracción	Abstraction	Colaboración	Collaboration
Acción	Action	Colección	Collection
Acusación	Accusation	Combinación	Combination
Adaptación	Adaptation	Compensación	Compensation
Admiración	Admiration	Composición	Composition
Aplicación	Application	Concentración	Concentration
Apreciación	Appreciation	Concepción	Conception
Asociación	Association	Condición	Condition
Aspiración	Aspiration	Conservación	Conservation
Atención	Attention	Consideración	Consideration
Atracción	Attraction	Constitución	Constitution
Autorización	Authorization	Construcción	Construction
Celebración	Celebration	Exposición	Exposition
Circulación	Circulation	Ficción	Fiction
Civilización	Civilization	Formación	Formation
Clasificación	Classification	Nación	Nation
		Simplificación	Simplification

The following near perfect cognates follow the rule for English adjectives ending **'ic'** can be converted to Spanish by replacing with an **'ico'**.

Académico	Academic	Electrónico	Electronic
Alcohólico	Alcoholic	Erótico	Erotic
Artístico	Artistic	Exótico	Exotic
Auténtico	Authentic	Fantástico	Fantastic
Automático	Automatic	Genérico	Generic
Básico	Basic	Genético	Genetic
Característico	Characteristic	Geométrico	Geometric
Clásico	Classic	Heroico	Heroic
Cómico	Comic	Irónico	Ironic
Democrático	Democratic	Mágico	Magic
Dinámico	Dynamic	Médico	Medic
Diplomático	Diplomatic	Mosaico	Mosaic
Doméstico	Domestic	Orgánico	Organic
Dramático	Dramatic	Pánico	Panic
Económico	Economic	Plástico	Plastic

The following near perfect cognates follow the rule for English adjectives ending **'ous'** can be converted to Spanish by replacing with an **'oso'**.

Curioso	Curious	Numeroso	Numerous
Delicioso	Delicious	Precioso	Precious
Glorioso	Glorious	Religioso	Religious
Misterioso	Mysterious	Tedioso	Tedious

The following near perfect cognates follow the rule for nouns ending **'ct'** in English can be converted to

Spanish by replacing with a **'cto'**.

Abstracto	Abstract	Correcto	Correct
Acto	Act	Exacto	Exact
Artefacto	Artefact	Excepto	Except
Compacto	Compact	Insecto	Insect
Conflicto	Conflict	Perfecto	Perfect
Contacto	Contact	Producto	Product

Day 6. False Cognates

A false cognate is a word that may look very similar to another one, but that doesn't mean the same thing. There are many false cognates between these two languages, so it is important to know a little more about them and pay close attention to their correct applications in order to avoid making mistakes.

There are too many samples for cognates to make an extensive list, but we can see some of these words below with little examples to keep in mind:

Spanish Word	English Cognate	Real Meaning
Actualmente	Actually	Nowadays
Advertencia	Advertising	Warning
Aviso	Advice	Notice
Asistir	Assist	To help
Billón	Billion	Trillion
Carpeta	Carpet	Folder
Chocar	Choke	To crash
Codo	Code	Elbow
Complacer	Complain	To please
Contestar	Contest	To answer
Decepción	Deception	Disappointment
Dinero	Dinner	Money
Embarazada	Embarrassed	Pregnant
Empresa	Empress	Company
Estimado	Estimate	Dear
Éxito	Exit	Success
Grosería	Grocery	Curse word
Idioma	Idiom	Language
Introducir	Introduce	To get in
Largo	Large	Long
Nudo	Nude	Knot
Pretender	Pretender	To intend
Media	Media	Sock
Realizar	Realize	To carry out
Recordar	Record	To remember
Ropa	Rope	Clothes
Sano	Sane	Healthy
Sensible	Sensible	Sensitive
Soportar	Support	To put up with
Suceso	Success	Event

Examples:

*Nadie cree en eso **actualmente**.*

Wrong translation: Nobody believes in that **actually**.

Correct translation: Nobody believes in that **nowadays**.

***Advertencia**: solo personal autorizado.*

Wrong translation: **Advertising**: Authorized personnel only.

Correct translation: **Warning**: Authorized personnel only.

*¡Busca el **éxito**, amigo mío!*

Wrong translation: Look for the **exit,** my friend!

Correct translation: Look for **success**, my friend!

*Ella está **embarazada** de ocho meses.*

Wrong translation: She is eight months **embarrassed**.

Correct translation: She is eight months **pregnant**.

*¿Tienes **dinero** para la cena?*

Wrong translation: Do you have **dinner** for dinner?

Correct translation: Do you have **money** for dinner?

*No lo **soporto** más.*

Wrong translation: I can't **support** it anymore.

Correct translation: I can't **put up** with it anymore.

*Está en la **carpeta** azul.*

Wrong translation: It's in the blue **carpet**.

Correct translation: It's in the blue **folder**.

Day 7. The Spanish Pronouns

In its most general definition, a pronoun it's a word that can take the place of a noun in a sentence. They are important because, as you know, we tend to use a subject in almost every single phrase we say, and the vast majority of those subjects are nouns.

Types Of Pronouns

In the following chart, we can find the typical uses of each type of pronoun in Spanish. In the next lessons, we'll be learning a little more about them, and we'll also see some sample sentences.

Types of Pronouns	
Personal	Substitute persons, places, or things
Demonstrative	Indicate a noun's time, space, and distance
Possessive	Demonstrate ownership
Indefinite	Doesn't refer to any person or thing in particular
Numeral	Specifies a quantity of a noun in form of a number
Relative	Introduces dependent (or **relative**) clauses in sentences
Interrogative	Is used to make asking questions easy
Enclitic	Unite with the word before them, forming a single word
Reflexive	Refers back to the subject of a sentence

Personal Pronouns

The personal pronouns in Spanish are shown in the chart below.

| | | Types of Personal Pronouns | | | | | |
		Spanish Subjective	English Subjective	Spanish Objective	English Objective	Spanish Possessive	English Possessive
S I N G U L A R	1st Person	Yo	I	Mí	Me	Mio	Mine
	2nd Person (Informal)	Tú, vos	You	Ti, vos	You	Tuyo	Yours
	2nd Person (Formal)	Usted	You	Usted	You	Suyo	Yours
	3rd Person (Masculine)	Él	He	Él	Him	Suyo	His
	3rd Person (Feminine)	Ella	She	Ella	Her	Suyo	Her
P L U R A L	1st Person (All inclusive)	Nosotros	We	Nosotros	Us	Nuestro	Our
	1st Person (Masculine)	Nosotros	We	Nosotros	Us	Nuestro	Our
	1st Person (Feminine)	Nosotras	We	Nosotras	Us	Nuestra	Our
	2nd Person (Masculine)	Vosotros	You	Vosotros	You	Vuestro	Your
	2nd Person (Feminine)	Vosotras	You	Vosotras	You	Vuestro	Your
	2nd Person (All inclusive)	Ustedes	You	Ustedes	You	Suyo	Your
	3rd Person (All inclusive)	Ellos	They	Ellos	Them	Suyo	Their
	3rd Person (Masculine)	Ellos	They	Ellos	Them	Suyo	Their
	3rd Person (Feminine)	Ellas	They	Ellas	Them	Suyo	Their

From this chart, it is evident that every English pronoun has its Spanish equivalent and vice versa, but there are some features Spanish has that are quite different from English:

- There are formal and informal forms for the 2nd person singular in Spanish. They are to be used depending on the social situation where you are, who you are talking to, and even the courtesy manners of the people you're speaking to.

- The informal 2nd person of singular can be said in two ways: Tú and Vos. This is a dialectal difference. That is to say, depending on where you are from, you are more likely to use one form or the other. Example: A Venezuelan will likely say Tú and an Argentinian to say Vos.

- Because of the fact that almost all of the Spanish nouns have grammatical gender, the pronouns, adjectives, and articles to use will vary according to that gender. It is expected from the speaker to use the correct pronoun for every noun and is very intuitive, too, as you'll learn while you progress on the book.

- Another big difference is the use of two different forms for the 2nd person plural: Vosotros y Ustedes. The reason why there are two forms is a very interesting story, but the takeaway is this: Latin Americans use Ustedes, and Spaniards use Vosotros. Everybody on both sides of the pond understands the two forms perfectly, but it is customary to use the one they learn as a kid.

Day 8. Demonstrative Pronouns

Sometimes, names say it all. These are pronouns (words used to substitute other words as we speak in order to avoid unnecessary repetitions) that are used to show or demonstrate (yeah, you guessed that by the name, didn't you?) things, animals or persons.

They indicate the relative distance between two objects, or between an object and a person, between to persons, between an animal and a person. I think you get the idea.

These pronouns can be of three different degrees depending on the distance they have from the person speaking, as you can see from the table below where the main demonstrative pronouns in Spanish and their usual English equivalents are listed:

Degree	Masculine Singular	Feminine Singular	Masculine Plural	Feminine Plural	Neutral
First	Este (This)	Esta (This)	Estos (These)	Estas (These)	Esto (These)
Second	Ese (That)	Esa (That)	Esos (Those)	Esas (Those)	Eso (Those)
Third	Aquel (That)	Aquella (That)	Aquellos (Those)	Aquellas (Those)	Aquellos (Those)

Examples:

A. First Degree:

- *Este helado está sabroso.*
  This ice cream is tasty.
- *Esto se llama tenedor.*
  This is called a fork.
- *Esta ropa es barata.*
  These clothes are cheap.
- *Estos juguetes son bonitos.*
  These toys are beautiful.
- *Estas cucharillas están sucias.*
  These spoons are dirty.

B. Second Degree:

- *Ese camión es muy grande.*

  That truck is too big.

- *Eso no es un teléfono.*

  That is not a phone.

- *Esa no es tu mascota.*

  That is not your pet.

- *Esos libros son un regalo.*

  Those books are a gift.

- *Esas tazas son de tú tío.*

  Those cups belong to your uncle.

C. Third Degree:

- *Aquel edificio es muy antiguo.*

  That building is very old.

- *Aquella puerta no está cerrada.*

  That door is not closed.

- *Aquello parece usado.*

  That looks used.

- *Aquellos arboles parecen morir.*

  Those trees seem to die.

It's important to note that the distance between the object and the speaker can be a physical distance or a time distance.

Another important takeaway here is that sometimes you can confuse the demonstrative pronoun "este" with one of the conjugation forms of the verb "estar"; how to know which one is being used? My recommendation would **always be to pay attention to the context**.

Day 9. Possessive Pronouns

Possessive pronouns are those used to indicate possession, belonging, or any narrow relationship between and entity and a grammatical person. They should match in gender and number with the thing possessed and are always used after the noun.

The following table shows a quick summary of the most frequently used possessive pronouns in Spanish.

Person	Singular	Plural
First	Mío, Míos, Mía, Mías (Mine)	Nuestro, Nuestros, Nuestra, Nuestras (Ours)
Second	Tuyo, Tuyos, Tuya, Tuyas (Yours)	Vuestro, Vuestra, Vuestros, Vuestras De Ustedes (Yours)
Third (Male)	Suyo, Suyos (His)	Suyos, De Ellos (Theirs)
Third (Female)	Suya, Suyas (Hers)	Suyas, De Ellas (Theirs)
Third (Neutral)	Suyo (Its)	-----

Examples:

- *Ese carro es **mío**.*

That car is **mine**.

- *Esos zapatos son **míos**.*
  Those shoes are **mine**.

- *Aquí está **tu** pulsera, ¿dónde está la **mía**?*
  Here is **your** bracelet, where is **mine**?

- *Este libro es **tuyo**.*
  This book is **yours**.

- *Esa es **mi** tarjeta de crédito, no **tuya**.*
  That is **my** credit card, not **yours**.

- *¿Son **tuyas** esas franelas?*
  Are those t-shirts all **yours**?

- *Le presté **mi** carro a John y el me prestó el **suyo**.*
  I lent John **my** car, and he lent me **his**.

- *Jack fue al supermercado, esas manzanas son **suyas**.*
  Jack went to the supermarket; those apples are **his**.

- *Yo no pude comprar el carro, mi mamá me dio el **suyo**.*
  I couldn't buy the car; my mother gave me **hers**.

- ***Su** país es caluroso, el **nuestro** es frio.*
  Your country is hot, and **ours** is cold.

- *María y yo fuimos a la playa con unos amigos* **nuestros**.

  Maria and I went to the beach with some friends of **ours**.

- **Nuestro** *idioma es difícil, el* **suyo** *es práctico*.

  Our language is difficult, and **yours** is practical.

Day 10. Indefinite Pronouns 1

These pronouns are those whose reference is not definite, and it only specifies the belonging to a certain class. They refer to being in an imprecise way. They can express quantity, diversity, equality, quality, distribution, and some other aspects that a being could have. These pronouns also can work as an adjective or adverb

Let's see them one by one with some examples in order to better understand what they're all about

Algo (something): it's neutral and used in affirmative phrases. It expresses an indeterminate or non-existing amount. Examples:

- *¿Joseph, quieres algo?*
  Joseph, do you want something?
- *¿Hay algo debajo de la mesa?*
  Is there something below the table?

Alguien (somebody or someone): It always refers to people. Not to be used for things or animals. Examples:

- *¿Estás buscando a alguien?*
  Are you looking for someone?
- *Yo necesito alguien que maneje un carro.*
  I need somebody who drives a car

Algunos, algunas, algún (some): It refers to people or things in an undetermined way. Examples:

- *En la fiesta había algunos amigos.*
  At the party there were some friends
- *Dentro del carro había algunas frutas.*
  Inside the car, there were some fruits
- *Algún libro comprarás.*
  You will buy some book.

Cada (every; each): It has no variations. It expresses distribution. Examples:

- *Cada niño recibió una computadora.*

Each kid received a computer.

- *Yo pago renta cada mes.*
  I pay rent every month.

Cualquier, cualquiera (any, anyone, anybody, and anything): It also has no variation. It expresses indifference or apathy. Examples:

- *Necesito cualquier medicina.*
  I need any medicine.
- *Necesito a cualquiera que me lleve al aeropuerto.*
  I need anyone to take me to the airport.

Day 11. Indefinite Pronouns 2

Demás (the rest): It designates the elements of a set that haven`t been mentioned or the unnamed part of a whole. It expresses diversity or variety. Example:

- *¿Dónde están los demás?*
  Where are the rest?
- *No te preocupes por lo demás.*
  Do not worry about the rest.

Demasiado or **demasiados** (too or too much): it indicates that the action denoted by the verb occurs at an intensity or degree level greater than necessary, which was expected or considered appropriate. Examples:

- *Tenemos demasiada agua en casa.*
  We have too much water at home.
- *Tu miedo es demasiado grande.*
  Your fear is too big.

Diferente (different): it indicates that it's not the

same, it doesn't look like the others or rest, it has different characteristics or qualities. Examples:

- *Hay diferentes opiniones sobre ese tema.*
  There are different opinions on that theme.
- *Tu trabajo es diferente al mío.*
  Your job is different than mine.

Igual or **mismo** (same, equal): It indicates it has the same nature, quantity, quality, value or form as other or other people or things, or that it shares with them common or similar qualities or characteristics. Examples:

- *Tú y yo cometimos el mismo error.*
  You and I made the same mistake.
- *Ambos equipos son iguales.*
  Both teams are equal.

Nadie (no one, nobody): It is used to refer people only, not for things or animals. Examples:

- *No tengo a nadie que haga el trabajo.*

I have no one to do the job.

- *Nadie vino al cementerio.*

  Nobody came to the cemetery.

Day 12. Numeral Pronouns And Numbers In General

Numbers are used to indicate quantities, and as pronouns, they're also used to indicate the amount of a noun, animal, or thing they represent. Numbers can come in several shapes and types, but for this book not to become a mathematical textbook, we'll classify them into five groups: cardinals, ordinals, distributives, partitives, and multiplying.

Cardinal numbers: they indicate the number or quantity of elements of a group no matter if it's amount is finite or infinite.

0	Cero (Zero)		
1	Uno, Un O Una (One)	11	Once (Eleven)
2	Dos (Two)	12	Doce (Twelve)
3	Tres (Three)	13	Trece (Thirteen)
4	Cuatro (Four)	14	Catorce (Fourteen)
5	Cinco (Five)	15	Quince (Fifteen)
6	Seis (Six)	16	Dieciséis (Sixteen)
7	Siete (Seven)	17	Diecisiete (Seventeen)
8	Ocho (Eight)	18	Dieciocho (Eighteen
9	Nueve (Nine)	19	Diecinueve (Nineteen)
10	Diez (Ten)	20	Veinte (Twenty)

From twenty, you form the numbers by adding the units from 1 to 9 as a suffix at the end of the word, in a similar fashion as we do in English:

21 Veintiuno	(twenty-one)
22 Veintidós	(twenty-two)
23 Veintitrés	(twenty-three)
24 Veinticuatro	(twenty-four)
25 Veinticinco	(twenty-five)
26 Veintiséis	(twenty-six)
27 Veintisiete	(twenty-seven)
28 Veintiocho	(twenty-eight)
29 Veintinueve	(twenty-nine)

Now, counting by ten:

30 Treinta	(Thirty)
40 Cuarenta	(Forty)
50 Cincuenta	(Fifty)
60 Sesenta	(Sixty)
70 Setenta	(Seventy)
80 Ochenta	(Eighty)
90 Noventa	(Ninety)
100 Cien	(One-hundred)

And the hundreds are formed by adding the suffix *cientos* at the end of the numbers: doscientos (two hundred), trescientos (three hundred), cuatrocientos (four hundred), quinientos (five hundred), seiscientos (six hundred), setecientos (seven hundred), ochocientos (eight hundred) novecientos (nine hundred).

The thousands, millions, etc. are formed just like the hundreds.

Day 13. Ordinal Numbers

Ordinal numbers allow us to express the order or position that an element occupies. In short, they are the words we use to say which position takes an element within an ordered series of things, animals, or persons.

1º   Primero (First)
2º   Segundo (Second)
3º   Tercero (Third)
4º   Cuarto (Fourth)
5º   Quinto (Fifth)
6º   Sexto (Sixth)
7º   Séptimo (Seventh)
8º   Octavo (Eighth)
9º   Noveno (Ninth)
10º Décimo (Tenth)

From here on, they are just added as in English:

11º Décimo Primero (Eleventh)
12º Décimo Segundo (Twelfth)
13º Décimo Tercero (Thirteenth)
14º Décimo Cuarto (Fourteenth)
15º Décimo Quinto (Fifteenth)
16º Décimo Sexto (Sixteenth)
17º Décimo Séptimo (Seventeenth)
18º Décimo Octavo (Eighteenth)
19º Décimo Novena (Nineteenth)

Counting by ten: vigésimo (twentieth), trigésimo (thirtieth), cuadragésimo (fortieth), and so on.

Examples:

- *Esta es mi primera guitarra.*
  This is my first guitar.
- *El segundo lugar pertenece a tu padre.*
  The second place belongs to your father.
- *Es la tercera vez que repito esto.*
  It's the third time I repeat this.
- *El cuarto bombillo a la derecha.*
  The fourth light bulb to the right.
- *El quinto marcador de la temporada.*
  The fifth score of the season.
- *Ella es la sexta de la lista.*
  She is the sixth on the list.
- *Mi séptima canción del año.*
  My seventh song of the year.
- *He votado por octava vez.*
  I've voted for the eighth time.
- *El noveno país que he visitado.*

The ninth country I have visited.

- *La décima naranja que me he comido.*
  The tenth orange I have eaten.

Distributive numbers: they indicate groups of individuals and distribute the core of the nominal syntagma. Its purpose is to make a distribution.

Examples:

- *Ambos merecen ese trabajo.*
  Both of you deserve that job.

Partitive numbers: they indicate quantities from the fractions or parts into which a unit or element is divided.

Examples:

- *Necesito la mitad de tus ahorros.*
  I need half of your savings.
- *Es una tubería de tres cuartos de pulgada.*

It's a tube of three-quarters of an inch.

Multiplying numbers: are those that express the number of times a certain thing is given or repeated. That is, they express a multiplication.

Examples:

- *Él tuvo una doble ocasión de comprar el apartamento.*

  He had a double occasion to buy the apartment.
- *Tengo un doble compromiso para hoy.*

  I have a double commitment today.

Day 14. Relative Pronouns

Relative pronouns are a type of pronoun which refers to a previous reference or background. They refer to a previously mentioned noun in the sentence which is called background. They are used to join two clauses. The second one, whose function is to qualify the subject of the first one. The most common relative pronouns in Spanish are:

Que: It's the most frequently used one because it refers to both people and things. It can be the subject or complement of its clause. Examples:

- *El hombre que está allí es mi hermano.*
  The man who is there is my brother.

El que, los que, la que, las que: these words refer to a name already mentioned and are used to avoid repeating the noun. Examples:

- *¿Tomaste el examen de español?*
  Respuesta: no, el que tome era matemáticas.

Did you take the Spanish test?

Answer: no, the one I took was of mathematics.

- *¿De qué países son esos carros?*

  Respuesta: los que ves aquí son de italia y los de allá son de alemania.

  Which countries are those cars from?

  Answer: the ones you see here are from Italy and the ones over there are from Germany.

- *¿Tienes pintura roja?*

  Respuesta: No, la que tengo es verde.

  Do you have red paint?

  Answer: no, the one I have is green.

- *¿Son americanas esas mujeres?*

  Respuesta: las que hablan entre sí lo son, las otras no.

  Are those women American?

  Answer: the ones speaking to each other are, the others are not.

Lo que: it is used to refer to ideas, actions, or concepts. It never is used to refer to nouns. Examples:

- *Lo que necesito es más tiempo.*

What I need is more time.

- *Perdí mi reloj, lo que me entristece.*
  I lost my watch, which makes me be sad.

- *¿Recuerdas lo que te dije ayer?*
  Do you remember what I told you yesterday?

Quien, quienes: they are used only to refer human beings and in parenthetic clauses. Examples:

- *Mi tío, que era escritor, vivió en México.*
  My uncle, who was a writer, lived in Mexico.

- *Esos hombres, quienes están en el balcón son millonarios.*
  Those men, who are in the balcony, are millionaires.

El cual, los cuales, la cual, las cuales: the use of these pronouns is generally limited to a sense of formality. It can be substituted in most cases. Examples:

- *Ningún alumno salió bien en el examen, el cual fue difícil.*

No student did well on the exam, which was difficult.

- *Se le presentó una carta, la cual aceptó.*
  He was presented a letter, which he accepted.
- *Las cosas, por las cuales luchamos se perdieron.*
  The things which we fight for are lost.

Cuyo, cuyos, cuya, cuyas: these pronouns denote possession. They always maintain agreement with the possession and never with the possessor. Examples:

- *La mujer, cuyo hijo viste pantalones negros, es venezolana.*
  The woman, whose son wears black pants, is a Venezuelan.
- *El hijo, cuyos padres sean ricos, será rico también.*
  The son, whose parents are rich, will be rich too.
- *El alumno, cuya madre trabaja en un restaurante, se llama Miguel.*
  The student, whose mother works in a restaurant, is called Miguel.
- *Juan, cuyas hermanas son muy hermosas.*

Juan, whose sisters are very beautiful.

Donde: it is a relative pronoun that makes reference to a place or location. Examples:

- *El pueblo donde yo crecí, es ahora una ciudad.*
  The town where I grew up is now a city.
- *La escuela donde voy queda en la calle 2.*
  The school I attend is in Street 2.

Day 15. Interrogative Pronouns

The interrogative pronouns designate beings or things whose identity or quantity is to be determined, and they are used to formulate direct questions about people, animals, or things. They always carry an accent mark in order to differentiate them from the relative pronouns. The following chart shows the most commonly used interrogative pronouns in Spanish and their English translations

Interrogative Pronouns	
¿Qué?	What?
¿Quién(es)?	Who? (singular or plural)
¿De quién(es)?	Whose? (singular or plural)
¿Con quién(es)?	With whom? (singular or plural)
¿Cómo?	How?
¿Dónde?	Where?
¿De dónde?	Whence?
¿Adónde?	Where?
¿Cuándo?	When?
¿Cuánto/-a/-os/-as?	How many? How much?
¿Por qué?	Why?
¿Cuál(es)?	Which? (singular or plural)

The pronoun *Qué* (What) is used to make questions

about things, and it always requests an explanation or definition. It can also be accompanied by a preposition like *de* or *para*.

- *¿**Qué** es eso?*
  What is that?
- *¿Para **qué** quieres el vaso?*
  What do you want the glass for?
- *¿**Qué** hora es?*
  What time is it?
- *¿**Qué** quieres comer?*
  What do you want to eat?

The pronouns ***Quién*** and ***Quiénes*** (Who) are always used to formulate questions about one or several people. The difference between them is that *Quién* is used for singular (just one person), and *Quiénes* is used for several people.

- *¿**Quiénes** llamaron?*
  Who called?

- *¿Con **quién** estás hablando?*
  Who are you talking to?

- *¿**Quiénes** son ellos?*
  Who are they?

- *¿**Quién** es tu madre?*
  Who is your mother?

The pronouns ***Cuál*** or ***Cuáles*** (which, in singular or plural) always request specific and predetermined information, as when you're making a selection from a list. They can be used for any gender, and the difference between them is that *Cuál* is used for singular (just one option), and *Cuáles* is used for several options.

- *¿**Cuál** es tu libro?*
  Which is your book?

- *¿**Cuál** de los dos cuadernos?*
  Which one of these two notebooks?

- *¿**Cuáles** son tus juguetes?*
  Which are your toys?

- *¿**Cuáles** zapatos son más bonitos?*

  Which shoes are more beautiful?

The pronoun **Cuánto**, with its female version **Cuánta** and their plurals **Cuántos** and **Cuántas,** are used to ask about quantities. Unlike in English, these pronouns are used indistinctively for countable and uncountable quantities. These pronouns should be matched in gender and number with the noun they modify in a given sentence.

- *¿**Cuántos** países hay?*

  How many countries are there?

- *¿**Cuánto** dinero tienes?*

  How much money do you have?

- *¿**Cuánto** agua hay en el tanque?*

  How much water is there in the tank?

- *¿**Cuánto** azúcar debo traer?*

  How much sugar should I bring?

- *¿**Cuántas** veces quieres que te lo diga?*

  How many times do you want me to say it?

Day 16. Enclitic Pronouns

That's a really funny name, isn't it? Enclitic? What's that all about?

Well, we need to know some linguistics in order to understand in layman's terms this concept. It goes something like this:

There are some words or *morphemes* that never seem to mean anything because they usually go before or after another word and modify its meaning. They are called the *clitics* and, in general, belong to one of two types: *proclitic* (when they appear before the associated word) and *enclitic* (when they go after the associated word).

But that's not the end. In everyday speak, we tend to speak faster and faster as the time goes by (that happens in both English and Spanish), so these little words or clitics get absorbed into their associated words in order to form new words, as in the case of the contractions (aren't, you've, don't, etc.)

So, we now know enough to understand better that enclitic pronouns are, by definition, pronouns that join the preceding word in order to form a single, new word.

The Spanish enclitic pronouns are *me, te, se, lo, los, la, las, le, les, nos y os,* and you'll see what they mean on the following examples.

Examples:

- *Quiero comer la naranja. = Quiero comer**la**.*
  I want to eat the orange. = I want to eat it.
- *La pretende amar. = Pretende amar**la**.*
  He pretends to love her. = He pretends loving her.
- *Lo está cambiando. = Está cambiándo**lo**.*
  He is changing it. = He is changing it.
- *Lo consiguió poner. = Consiguió poner**lo**.*

He found out how to put it. = He found out how to put it.

- *Lo estuvo escribiendo. = Estuvo escribiéndo**lo**.*
  He had been writing it. = He had been writing it.
- *Lo puedes abrir y cerrar. = Puedes abrir**lo** y cerrar**lo**.*
  You can open it and close it. = You can open it and close it.

When you're speaking in the imperative mode, that is, giving commands for other people to execute the actions you need to be done, most of the Spanish verbs need to add an enclitic pronoun at the end.

- *¡Ábrelo!*
  Open it!
- *En el refrigerador hay una manzana, cómetela.*
  There's an apple in the fridge, eat it.

Day 17. Reflexive Pronouns

When there's an action on a sentence that the subject is performing on himself, herself: that's when reflexive pronouns come in handy. These kinds of pronouns are generally used with pronominal verbs and are way more common in Spanish than they are in English.

Reflexive pronouns always coincide with the subject's grammatical gender and number and are placed right before the verb in a sentence.

The reflexive pronouns in Spanish are shown on the table below:

Personal Pronoun	Reflexive Pronoun
Yo	Me
Tú	Te
Él Ella Ud.	Se
Nosotros	Nos
Vosotros	Os
Ellos Ellas Uds.	Se

Examples:

- *Yo me compré una casa.*
  I bought a house for myself.
- *Me quiero ir del país.*
  I want to leave the country.
- *Tú te fuiste tarde.*
  You left late.
- *¿Te acuerdas de Ricardo?*
  Do you remember Ricardo?
- *Él se fracturó el codo.*
  He fractured his arm.
- *Ella se comió un helado.*
  She ate ice cream.
- *Usted se ve linda.*
  You look pretty.
- *¿Vos te recuerda de Juan?*
  Do you remember Juan?
- *Nosotros nos divertimos bastante.*
  We enjoyed quite a bit.
- *Nosotras nos quedamos.*
  We'll stay.
- *Vosotros os iréis mañana.*

You'll go tomorrow.

- *Ellos se han levantado.*

  They have stood up.

- *Ellas se fueron a pasear un rato.*

  They went on a walk for a while.

- *Ustedes se quedaron en casa.*

  You stayed home.

- *Yo me traje la chaqueta.*

  I brought my jacket.

- *Tú te contentaste por la comida.*

  You got happy for the food.

- *Él se quiere ir a México.*

  He wants to go to Mexico.

- *Ella se quejó de la comida.*

  She complained about the food.

- *Usted se ha perdido.*

  You've gotten lost.

- *Nosotros nos iremos a la ciudad.*

  We'll leave for the city.

- *Nosotras nos arrepentimos de lo que hicimos.*

  We regret what we did.

Day 18. The Spanish Articles

The Articles are those words that precede the nouns in a sentence in order to refer to them and give some extra information like their grammatical number (if the noun is in singular or plural) and grammatical gender (we'll learn more about it on the next lesson).

As in English, there are two types of articles in Spanish:

Definite Articles

Definite articles are used when the speaker knows about the noun that goes after these articles. The following chart shows how to use them according to the grammatical number and gender of the nouns:

	Masculine	Feminine	Neutral
Singular	El	La	Lo
Plural	Los	Las	

Examples:

- *La casa*

  The house

- *Los niños*

  The Children

- *El hombre*

  The man

- *Los perros*

  The Dogs

- *Las mujeres*

  The women

- *Los hombres*

  The men

Indefinite Articles

This kind of article is used when the speaker does not know, or it's not sure about the noun and barely knows some info about its grammatical number. The following chart shows how to use indefinite articles:

	Masculine	Feminine
Singular	Un	Una
Plural	Unos	Unas

Examples:

- *Un niño*
  A boy
- *Una puerta*
  A door
- *Unos tomates*
  Some tomatoes
- *Unas bananas*
  Some bananas

See how these sentences are used to express the person speaking does not know specific information about the subject: They're speaking about a random boy, a random girl, and some tomatoes / bananas, but only without determining how many of them are in place.

Yes, you read right: there are also indefinite plural articles in Spanish too.

Day 19. Types Of Words

Derivatives

As you know by now, Spanish is a romance language, formed in what we know today as Spain, specifically the region of Castile, from the gradual degradation of the Classic Latin into a vulgar form called Vulgar Latin.

During the early stages of the formation of the Spanish language, it received a wide variety of lexical influences from many disparate origins, such as Greek, Germanic, Arabic, from other romance languages, etc.

These kinds of words that have primitive origins and have been incorporated into modern Spanish are commonly known as *Primitive words* and tend to form the majority of what we call today *Root Words*.

Modern words in Spanish are in big part composite words, which are formed by taking a root and adding a derivation (or lexical variant) in order to modify that root and give it some additional grammatical information such as gender, number, person, tense, mode, etc.

Let's take a look at some examples to clarify what's been said:

Root Word: Agua (Water)

Derivatives: acuático (aquatic), acueducto (aqueduct), acuífero (aquifer), acuoso (aqueous), aguacero (downpour), aguada (watery), aguado (watery), aguador (water carrier), aguafiestas (spoiler), aguardiente (spirits), aguaje (fake), paraguas (umbrella), piragua (canoe)

Root Word: Habitar (inhabit)

Derivatives: cohabitación (cohabitation), cohabitar (co-habitat), deshabitado (inhabited), deshabitar (uninhabit), habitabilidad (habitability), habitable (inhabitable), habitación (habitation), habitáculo (cabin), habitante (inhabitant), inhabitable.

These are only two examples of the literally thousands of root words and derivatives that are possible in Spanish. It seems like an impossible task to learn them all!!!

But it's not so difficult if **you understand the process of forming derivatives words**.

There are mainly two ways of forming derivative words:

Prefixation: new words are formed by adding a prefix to the root. Example:

Anteojo = Prefix *Ante* + Root *ojo*

Suffixation: new words are formed by adding a suffix to the root. Example:

Facilidad = Root *Fácil* + Suffix *dad*

It is important to note that while prefixation is simply merging the prefix and root together to form a new word, suffixation in Spanish sometimes requires adaptation of the suffix according to the type of word to form.

Knowing about this new word-forming process is important because it will help you leverage the existing vocabulary, you have to help you continue building your knowledge and develop your Spanish speaking skills. So, if you consider words like the perfect cognates, for example, use them as a base and begin forming new words as needed, you'll be learning fast along the way and gain interesting communication tools as you go.

In order to help you learn more about this word-formation process, the next chapters are going to go a little deeper on the building blocks for those new words: prefixes and suffixes. Each one of those modifies the meaning of a word in many different ways, and maybe when you hear a new word with a known suffix or prefix, you'll be able to know in advance (always paying attention to the context) what the speaker is talking about

Day 20. Spanish Prefixes

A prefix is a word or a group of letters that is placed before another word called root in order to give it an additional meaning. You can find some of the Spanish prefixes, meanings, and examples below:

Prefix	Meaning	Examples
Ante	Indicates Precedence	Antesala (Preview), Anteojos (Eyeglasses)
Contra	Opposite Position	Contragolpe (Counter Strike)
Entre	Intermediate Position	Entrelíneas (Between Lines)
Extra	Something External	Extraterrestre (Extraterrestrial), Extraordinario (Extraordinary)
Infra	Inferior Position	Infrahumano (Infrahuman), Infraestructura (Infrastructure)
Inter	Posición Intermedia	Internacional (International), Interfaz (Interface)
Pos	After	Posdental (Post dental), Posverbal (Postverbal)
Pre	Before	Predorsal (Predorsal), Premolar (Premolar)
Re	Repetition	Recámara (Bedroom), Reflujo (Reflux)
Retro	Backwards	Retro propulsor (Retro propulsor), Retroceder (To Go Back)
Sobre/Super	Posición Superior	Sobrevalorar (Overvalue)
Sub	Under	Suburbano (Suburban), Subyacer (Underlie)
Supra	Higher Position	Supranacional (Supranational)
Tele	Long Distance	Telecomunicaciones (Telecommunications), Telégrafo (Telegraph)
Tra(n)s	To the Other Side Of	Trasfondo, Transatlántico (Transatlantic)
Tra(n)s + Verb	To Continue Going After Reaching A Limit	Traspasar (Transpose), Trasplantar (Transplant), Transformar (Transform)
Ultra	Beyond Limits	Ultramar (Ultramar), Ultratumba (Afterlife)
Auto	About Oneself	Autocrítica (Self-Critical), Autodidacta (Self-Taught)

Prefix	Meaning	Examples
Co-/Con-/Com	Indicates Collectivity	Coautor (Coauthor), Consuegro (The Father in Law of Your Son or Daughter), Compadre (The Godfather of Your Son or Daughter)
Bi	Two or Double	Bilateral (Bilateral), Binóculo (Binoculars), Bilingüe (Bilingual)
Hiper	Excessive	Hiperactivo (Hyperactive), Hipertenso (Hypertensive)
Hipo	Deficient	Hipotermia (Hypothermia), Hipoglicemia (Hypoglycemia)
Macro	Really Big	Macro concierto (Macro concert), Macro fiesta (Macro party)
Micro	Really Small	Microchip (Microchip), Microcrédito (Microcredit)
Mono	One or Only	Monocultivo (Monoculture), Monólogo (Monologue)
Multi	Several	Multivitamina (Multivitamin), Multicultural (Multicultural)
Nano	Really, Really Small	Nanosegundo (Nanosecond), Nanotecnología (Nanotechnology)
Pluri	Plural	Pluriempleado (Moonlighter), Pluridimensional (Multi-dimensional)
Poli	Several	Polivalente (Multipurpose), Políglota (Polyglot)
Requeté	Repetition	Requetelimpio (Very, Very Clean)
Semi	Mitad o Imperfecto	Semicírculo (Semicircle), Semiprofesional (Semiprofessional), Semiconsciente (Semiconscious)
Sobre/Super	Abundant or Excessive	Sobrenatural (Supernatural), Sobreactuar (Overreact)
Tri	Three	Trimestre (Trimester), Trípode (Tripod)
Uní	One or Only	Unicolor (Unicolor), Unidireccional (Unidirectional), Unicejo (A Person Whose Eyebrows Are Merged into One)
A-/An	Opposite Of	Atípico (Atypical), Anormal (Abnormal)
Anti	Against	Antisistema (Antisystem), Antigripal (Anti Flu), Antivirus (Antivirus)
Des	Opposite Of	Desleal (Disloyal), Desempleado (Unemployed)
I-/Im-/In	Opposite Of	Ilícito (Illicit), Irreal (Unreal), Imposible (Impossible), Inútil (Useless)

Day 21. Spanish Suffixes

A *suffix* is a letter or group of letters added at the end of a word that makes a new word. Depending on the type of word you add the suffix to, you can find the following categories:

Suffixes That Form Nouns

These suffixes are used in the formation of derivate words that will acquire a grammatical classification as nouns. They can be added to:

Adjectives: In order to form abstract concepts that indicate quality:

Suffix	Root Word – Derivate Word
-ancia	*Abundante* (Abundant) – *Abundancia* (Abundancy)
-anza	*Bueno* (Good) –*Bonanza* (Bonanza)
-ario	*Fácil* (Easy) –*Facilidad* (Ease)
-dad	*Sobrio* (Sober) – *Sobriedad* (Sobriety)
-encia	*Prudente* (Prudent) –*Prudencia* (Prudence)
-ería	*Tonto* (Fool) – *Tontería* (Foolishness)
-ez	*Sencillo* (Simple) – *Sencillez* (Simplicity)
-eza	*Ligero* (Light) – *Ligereza* (Lightness)
-ía	*Cortés* (Polite) –*Cortesía* (Politeness)
-idad	*Bárbaro* (Barbarian) –*Barbaridad* (Barbarity)
-or	*Verde* (Green) – *Verdor* (Greenness)
-tad	*Libre* (Free) –*Libertad* (Freedom)
-ud	*Sano* (Healthy) – *Salud* (Health)
-umbre	*Podrido* (Rotten) –*Podredumbre* (Rot)
-ura	*Blando* (Soft) –*Blandura* (Softness)

Verbs: in order to form abstract or concrete nouns, expressing an action, the result of an action, the agent, or the instrument.

Suffix	Root Word – Derivate Word
-Ada	*Bajar* (To Go Down) – *Bajada* (Descent)
-Ado	*Abonar* (To Pay For) – *Abonado* (Subscriber)
-Ador	*Labrar* (To Plow) – *Labrador* (Farmer)
-Adora	*Sembrar* (To Sow) – *Sembradora* (Sower)
-Adura	*Armar* (To Arm) – *Armadura* (Armor)
-Aje	*Embalar* (To Pack) – *Embalaje* (Packing)
-Ancia	*Estar* (To Be) – *Estancia* (Ranch)
-Ante	*Pasear* (To Take A Walk) – *Paseante* (Pedestrian)
-Anza	*Cobrar* (To Charge) – *Cobranza* (Collection)
-Ción	*Decir* (To Say) – *Dicción* (Diction)
-Dor	Comprar (To Buy) – Comprador (Buyer)
-Dura	*Tachar* (To Cross Out) – *Tachadura* (Erasure)
-Edura	*Barrer* (To Sweep) – *Barredura* (Sweepings)
-Encia	*Advertir* (To Warn) – *Advertencia* (Warning)
-Erío	*Gritar* (To Yell) - *Griterío* (Shouting)
-Ida	*Venir* (To Come) – *Venida* (Coming)
-Ido	*Sentir* (To Feel) – *Sentido* (Sense)
-Idura	*Escurrir* (To Drain) – *Escurridura* (Drag-Out)
-Ina	*Regañar* (To Scold) – *Regañina* (Scolding)
-Mento	*Armar* (To Arm) – *Armamento* (Weapons)
-Miento	*Vencer* (To Win) – *Vencimiento* (Expiration)
-Sión	*Conceder* (To Concede) – *Concesión* (Concession)
-Tor	*Esculpir* (To Sculpt) – *Escultor* (Sculptor)

Day 22. Adjectives

These words are used to describe the characteristics of a person, a thing or something in particular. It can also be defined as a word that describes or clarifies a noun.

This description could be about physical characteristics as in: the blue pants, the red shirt, the yellow cap; emotional characteristics as in: she is happy, he is upset; features that you can feel or see, as in: the cup is hot, it's dark or intangible characteristics as in: is old or is new.

There are many examples of Spanish about adjectives, just like:

- *La mesa blanca.*
  A white table.
- *Un cuadro bonito.*
  A cute painting.
- *Un buen hombre.*
  A good man.

- *Laura está triste.*

  Laura is sad.

- *¿Tienes el libro grande?*

  Do you have the big book?

- *Como en la vieja escuela.*

  As in the old school.

They can also be used in series, that is, they can appear in the same sentence and modify the subject in several ways.

- *Los zapatos negros nuevos están en la caja.*

  The new black shoes are on the box.

Day 23. Adverbs

An adverb is a word or phrase that modifies or qualifies an adjective, verb, or other adverb or a word group, expressing a relation of place, time, circumstance, manner, cause, degree, etc.

To better understand how the adverbs work, we should take a look at the chart below:

Type	Spanish	English
Places (Locations)	Aquí, ahí, allí, acá, allá, cerca, lejos, enfrente, detrás, dentro, fuera, arriba, encima, abajo, debajo, donde, adonde	Here, there, near, far, in front, back, inside, in, out, up, down, below, where, where
Time (Temporary)	Hoy, ayer, mañana, tarde, temprano, pronto, nunca, ahora, entonces, antes, después, anoche, siempre, bien	Today, Yesterday, tomorrow, afternoon, morning, soon, never, now, then, before, after, last night, then, always, well
Mode (Qualities)	Bien, mal, así, tal, despacio, aprisa, adrede, aún, como, peor, mejor	Well, evil, as well, such, slowly, quick, deliberately, yet, as, worse, better
Quantity (Quantitative)	Mucho, poco, algo, nada, muy, demasiado, medio, bastante, más, menos, casi, sólo, cuánto, todo	Much, little, something, anything, very, too much, half, a lot, more, less, almost, only, how much, everything
Affirmation (To affirm)	Sí, ciertamente, claro, desde luego	Yes, indeed, of course
Negation (To Deny)	No, nunca, jamás, tampoco, nada	No, never, ever, either, nothing
Doubt (Uncertainty)	Acaso, quizá, tal vez, posiblemente	Maybe, possibly

Prepositions

These words are frequently used to show the relation

between a substantive or pronoun and another part of the sentence. Among the most popular prepositions we can mention:

A	(to)
Ante	(Before, in light of)
Bajo	(Under)
Con	(With)
Contra	(Against)
De	(of, in, on, for, as, at, about, from, out of, by, made of, off, unto, to)
Desde	(From, since, as of)
En	(in)
Entre	(between, among, amongst, amidst, amid)
Hacia	(to, toward)
Hasta	(to, up to, until, 'til)
Para	(for, by, in order to, towards)
Por	(of, for, by, through, along, after, about, to, due to, via, around)
Según	(according to, by)
Sin	(without)
Así Que	(so)
Sobre	(over, above)
Tras	(after)

Examples:

- *Vamos **a** la playa.*

  Let's go to the beach.

- ***Ante** lo ocurrido anoche, prefiero quedarme.*

  In light of what happened last night, I rather to stay.

- *La temperatura en Chile puede caer **bajo** cero.*

  The temperature in Chile can go below zero.

Day 24. Conjunctions And Interjections

Conjunctions

These words are used to connect words, phrases, and clauses within sentences. They are classified in coordinated (elements of the same category together) and subordinated (introduce subordinate sentences that come together with a prayer independent).

Among them we can mention:

Y	(and)
O	(or)
Pero	(but)
Que	(that)
Porque	(because)
Si	(if)
Cuando	(when)

Now let's look at a couple of examples to understand better:

- *Los tuvieron a pan **y** agua.*
  They were only given bread and water.

- *El cielo muestra notables cambios en la mañana **y** en la noche.*

  The sky shows very noticeable changes between morning and night.
- *Mariana se quedó en casa **porque** quiere estudiar.*

  Mariana stayed home because she wants to study.

Interjections

Interjections are words used to express emotion, although they don't have a grammatical connection with the rest of the sentence.

In the list of interjections are:

- ¡Ah!
- ¡Hey!
- ¡Wow!
- ¡Vaya!
- ¡Caramba!

Examples:

- *¡Ah! Ahora lo recuerdo.*

  Ah! Now I remember.

- *Hey! Se te cayó algo al suelo.*

  Hey! You dropped something to the floor.

- *¡Que linda está tu casa, wow!*

  Your house is very pretty, wow!

- *¡Vaya! Con que esas tenemos.*

  All right! I can see what's going on.

Day 25. All Nouns Have Genders

I can almost hear you asking several questions; let's do a simple question/answer exercise for this lesson, ok?

Q: Ok, I understand there are masculine beings and feminine beings, like a man or a woman, a bull and a cow, etc. But what about inanimate things like a refrigerator, a box, or a flower? They are nouns and definitely don't have any genders.

A: Well, in Spanish, they do have genders. In fact, every noun has a gender in Spanish.

Q: Why is it? Where does this gender thing come from?

A: Simple, Spanish is a romance language, and thus it has inherited many of its features from Classic Latin or *Lingua Latina*. The other romance languages (Portuguese, French, Romanian, Italian, Catalan,

Sard, etc.) also share this feature, called "Grammatical Gender".

Q: Are nouns the only words that have genders?

A: No, nouns are not the only part of speech that has a gender in Spanish: articles, adverbs, participles, and pronouns also have grammatical gender. <u>They all change in a sentence depending on the gender of the noun.</u>

Q: How to know which gender to use for a given noun?

A: There are some simple rules:

a. If you're speaking about people, almost 99% of the times the grammatical gender is the same biological gender, especially when you're referring to a person's origin (The American would be "el Americano" or "la Americana" according to the person's sex) or occupation ("el doctor" or "la doctora")

b. If you're speaking about animals, the grammatical gender will not necessarily be related to the biological gender. For example: The turtle is "la tortuga" for both male and female, but the dog is "el perro" or "la perra", depending on the sex.

c. If you're speaking about inanimate things, then you better remember the gender to use, because it's chosen arbitrarily and only learn through practice.

Q: Can I figure out the gender by a noun's terminations?

A: Yes, you can! Just remember that:

a. The nouns that end in the letters **-n, -o, -r, -s, -e, or –l (NORSEL) are masculine**.

b. Some other masculine nouns end in -ma, -pa, or – ta.

c. Nouns ending in **-umbre, -ie, -ión, -dad, -tad,** or **–i are feminine**.

Q: What can I do to learn to use grammatical genders correctly?

A: Just do what babies do when learning to speak!

LISTEN and REPEAT

(Well, this is a book, so read and repeat then, you got it, right?)

In the beginning, the easiest patterns to catch are in the word endings. If the word ends in 'a', they will generally be considered feminine; if they end on 'o', they will generally be considered masculine.

If it's a plural you're talking about, remember to use masculine forms for those cases where you don't know if everybody is a male or not. Only use feminine forms if you're absolutely sure all of the members of the group you're talking about are females.

Take a look at some of the words from the list of basic words we used some lessons ago; this time, we're going to add the corresponding articles depending on the word's grammatical gender and number. Just by reading this list, you'll begin noticing the patterns for using the articles correctly.

El Hombre	The Man	El Lápiz	The Pencil
Los Hombres	The Men	El Bolígrafo	The Pen
La Mujer	The Woman	La Mesa	The Table
Las Mujeres	The Women	La Silla	The Chair
El Niño	The Boy	El Libro	The Book
La Niña	The Girl	El Agua	The Water
Los Niños	The Children	La Manzana	The Apple
Las Personas	The People	La Naranja	The Orange
El Bebé	The Baby	El Tomate	The Tomato
La Bebé	The Baby	La Banana	The Banana
La Casa	The House	El Helado	The Ice Cream
El Edificio	The Building	El Pan	The Bread
La Ventana	The Window	La Salsa de tomate	The Ketchup
La Puerta	The Door	El Arroz	The Rice
La Bicicleta	The Bicycle	La Computadora	The Computer
La Pelota	The Ball	La Calle	The Street
La Muñeca	The Doll	La Escuela	The School
El Árbol	The Tree	La Universidad	The University
La Flor	The Flower	El Blanco	The White
El Carro	The Car	El Negro	The Black
La Camioneta	The Truck	El Azul	The Blue
El Perro	The Dog	El Verde	The Green

Day 26. Action Words: The Verbs

Let's see what we have learned so far:

- When you read a sentence in Spanish, there's a 90% possibility the words are pronounced in the same way they're written. That's part of the beauty of the language!
- There are five vocalic sounds in Spanish: A, E, I, O, U.
- We learned the Spanish pronouns.
- We learned some basic words.
- We also learned that every noun has a gender, and have some tricks up our sleeves on how to work with them.

We can almost begin constructing simple phrases!

But there is a very important part of speech we haven't covered so far: the verbs. They're the action words in a sentence that describe what the subject is doing, so learning them is a top priority if you actually want to communicate in Spanish.

As in English, there are regular and irregular verbs. But in Spanish, there are a ton more irregular verbs than in English!

But don't worry, we'll learn about how to conjugate them later: We need to learn how to walk first and only then we can start to run!

The first verb we'll talk about is the verb 'to be', and it's double meaning in Spanish: they understand being in a different way than we do.

To Be Or To Be: That's The Question

In Spanish, the English verb "To be" is split up into two verbs that come to mean different things. One is used when talking about a permanent state of being and the other for temporary states.

So, when you are referring to an innate characteristic of a person, animal, thing, etc. you should use the verb "*Ser*" as for example:

- **Soy** *americano.*
  I'm an American.
- **Soy** *profesor.*
  I'm a teacher.
- **Eres** *una linda mujer.*
  You are a beautiful woman.
- *Él* **es** *un niño.*
  He is a boy.

On the other hand, the verb "*Estar*" is used to express a temporary state, that is to say, something that can change at any moment.

- **Estoy** *cansado.*
  I'm tired.

- ***Estamos*** *en Caracas.*

  We're in Caracas.

- *Ella* **está** *esperándote.*

  She is waiting for you.

Want a quick formula to remember the concept? It's as simple as: ***How you feel and where you are, that is when you use estar.***

Day 27. Conjugation Of The Verb "SER"

The conjugation of the verb "SER" in its simple present form, can be found on the following chart

S	1st Person	Yo (I)	Soy (am)
I N G U L A R	2nd Person (Informal)	Tú, vos (you)	Eres, Sos (are)
	2nd Person (Formal)	Usted (you)	Es (is)
	3rd Person (Masculine)	Él (he)	Es (is)
	3rd Person (Feminine)	Ella (she)	Es (is)
P L U R A L	1st Person (All inclusive)	Nosotros	Somos (are)
	1st Person (Masculine)	Nosotros	Somos (are)
	1st Person (Feminine)	Nosotras	Somos (are)
	2nd Person (Masculine)	Vosotros (you)	Sois (are)
	2nd Person (Feminine)	Vosotras (you)	Sois (are)
	2nd Person (All inclusive)	Ustedes (you)	Son (are)
	3rd Person (All inclusive)	Ellos (they)	Son (are)
	3rd Person (Masculine)	Ellos (they)	Son (are)
	3rd Person (Feminine)	Ellas (they)	Son (are)

Examples:

- *Yo **soy** Juan Carlos.*

  I'm Juan Carlos.

- *Tú **eres** americano.*

  You're an American.

- *Vos **sos** futbolista.*

  You are a football player.

- *Usted **es** abogado.*

  You are a lawyer.

- *Él **es** mi padre.*

  He is my father.

- *Ella **es** mi esposa.*

  She is my wife.

- *Nosotros **somos** españoles.*

  We are Spanish.

- *Juan y yo (José) **somos** hombres.*

  Juan and I (José) are men.

- *Nosotras, las mujeres, **somos** bellas.*

  We, women, are beautiful.

- *Vosotros, los británicos, **sois** muchos.*

  You, the British, are a lot.

- *Vosotras las niñas **sois** pequeñas.*

  You, the girls, are small.

- *Ustedes **son** de méxico.*

  You are from Mexico.

- *Ellos, los cubanos, **son** felices.*

  They, the Cubans, are happy.

- *Ellos **son** muy altos.*

  They are very tall.

- *Ellas, las niñeras, **son** jóvenes.*

  They, the babysitters, are young.

There are many instances when the verb to be is employed without using a pronoun, as in the following sentences:

- ***Soy** Daniela.*

  I'm Daniela.

- *¿Quién es él? **Es** Jesús.*

  Who is him? He's Jesus.

- ***Es** Josefina, la vecina.*

  She is Josefina, the neighbor.

- ***Somos** lo que comemos.*

  We're what we eat.

- *Son los demás los que deben aprender.*

  The others are the ones who must learn.

Day 28. Conjugation Of The Verb "ESTAR"

The conjugation of the verb "ESTAR" in its simple present form, can be found on the following chart:

S	1ˢᵗ Person	Yo (I)	Estoy (am)
I	2ⁿᵈ Person (Informal)	Tú, vos (you)	Estás (are)
N			
G	2ⁿᵈ Person (Formal)	Usted (you)	Está (are)
U			
L	3ʳᵈ Person (Masculine)	Él (he)	Está (is)
A			
R	3ʳᵈ Person (Feminine)	Ella (she)	Está (is)
	1ˢᵗ Person (All inclusive)	Nosotros	Estamos (are)
	1ˢᵗ Person (Masculine)	Nosotros	Estamos (are)
P	1ˢᵗ Person (Feminine)	Nosotras	Estamos (are)
L	2ⁿᵈ Person (Masculine)	Vosotros (you)	Estáis (are)
U	2ⁿᵈ Person (Feminine)	Vosotras (you)	Estáis (are)
R	2ⁿᵈ Person (All inclusive)	Ustedes (you)	Están (are)
A	3ʳᵈ Person (All inclusive)	Ellos (they)	Están (are)
L	3ʳᵈ Person (Masculine)	Ellos (they)	Están (are)
	3ʳᵈ Person (Feminine)	Ellas (they)	Están (are)

Examples:

- *Yo **estoy** en casa.*

  I'm home.

- *¿Tú **estás** loco?*

  Are you insane?

- *Vos **estás** en madrid.*

  You are in Madrid.

- *Usted **es** un adulto.*

  You are an adult.

- *Él **es** profesor.*

  He is a professor.

- *Ella **es** colombiana.*

  She is a Colombian.

- *Nosotros **estamos** en la playa.*

  We are on the beach.

- *Nosotras, Ana y María, **estamos** bien.*

  We, Ana y María, are ok.

- *Vosotros **estáis** en españa.*

  You are in Spain.

- *Vosotras, chicas, **estáis** embarazadas.*

  You, girls, are pregnant.

- *¿Los niños? **Están** jugando.*

  The boys? They are playing.

- *Las chicas **están** en casa.*

  The girls are at home.

As you might have noticed from the sentences above, the most common sentence structure in Spanish is:

Subject + Verb + Complement

The verbs "ser" and "estar" are so common for everyday speaking that it is absolutely necessary to learn how to use them correctly.

There are many other irregular verbs in Spanish, but we'll only focus on these two verbs for a start, in order to build our vocabulary and to be able to create basic sentences for communicating with people.

Day 29. Some Other Verbs

You'll find below a list of Spanish verbs in their infinitive form, along with their English translation. We'll be using them later to begin building simple phrases.

Abrir	To Open	Conocer	To Know
Amar	To Love	Contactar	To Contact
Aceptar	To Accept	Contar	To Count
Aconsejar	To Advise	Contar	To Tell
Afeitar	To Shave	Contestar	To Answer/To Reply
Agradecer	To Thank	Correr	To Run
Ahorrar	To Save (Money)	Costar	To Cost
Almorzar	To Have Lunch	Cuidar	To Look After
Alquilar	To Rent/To Hire	Dar	To Give
Anular	To Cancel	Decidir	To Decide
Añadir	To Add	Decir	To Say
Aprender	To Learn	Describir	To Describe
Aterrizar	To Land	Desear	To Wish
Ayudar	To Help	Despedir	To Dismiss
Bailar	To Dance	Dibujar	To Draw
Bajar	To Go Down	Dirigir	To Manage
Buscar	To Look For	Discutir	To Discuss
Cambiar	To Change	Disfrutar	To Enjoy
Caminar	To Walk	Dormir	To Sleep
Cerrar	To Close	Durar	To Last
Comer	To Eat	Enseñar	To Teach
Cantar	To Sing	Entender	To Understand
Cargar	To Load, To Charge	Entrar	To Enter
Cenar	To Have Dinner	Enviar	To Send
Cerrar	To Close	Enfadar	To Get Angry
Chocar	To Crash, To Collide	Enseñar	To Teach
Compartir	To Share	Entender	To Understand
Complacer	To Please	Entrar	To Enter
Comprar	To Buy	Entregar	To Hand Over
Conducir	To Drive	Enviar	To Send

Escribir	To Write	Prestar	To Lend
Escuchar	To Listen	Prevenir	To Prevent, To Warn
Esperar	To Wait For	Quejar	To Complain
Estudiar	To Study	Querer	To Like
Evitar	To Avoid	Querer	To Want
Fallar	To Fail	Recordar	To Remember
Fumar	To Smoke	Reír	To Laugh
Hablar	To Speak	Reparar	To Repair
Hacer	To Do, To Make	Repasar	To Revise
Informar	To Inform	Repetir	To Repeat
Introducir	To Introduce	Reponer	To Put Back
Investigar	To Research	Robar	To Steal
Invitar	To Invite	Romper	To Break
Ir	To Go	Saber	To Know (A Fact)
Llegar	To Arrive	Salir	To Leave
Llenar	To Fill	Saltar	To Jump
Llevar	To Carry	Salvar	To Save
Llorar	To Cry	Seguir	To Follow
Necesitar	To Need	Sentar	To Sit Down
Odiar	To Hate	Sentir	To Feel
Oír	To Hear	Servir	To Serve
Olvidar	To Forget	Sonreír	To Smile
Organizar	To Organize	Tener	To Have
Parar	To Stop	Tirar	To Throw
Parecer	To Seem	Tocar	To Touch
Patinar	To Skate	Torcer	To Twist
Pedir	To Ask	Trabajar	To Work
Pegar	To Stick	Traer	To Bring
Pensar	To Think	Usar	To Use
Perder	To Lose	Utilizar	To Use
Perdonar	To Forgive	Vender	To Sell
Permitir	To Allow	Venir	To Come
Poder	To Be Able To	Ver	To See
Poner	To Put	Verificar	To Check
Preferir	To Prefer	Visitar	To Visit
Preguntar	To Ask	Vivir	To Live
		Volver	To Return

Day 30. Conjugation Of Regular Verbs

Did you notice any pattern in the verb list of the last lesson?

Because there is certainly something that comes out when you take a closer look at that list: *every single one of those verbs ends in one of three terminations: -AR, -ER, and -IR.*

This is very important to note because, the regular verbs in Spanish are formed by a root + termination, as for example:

Hablar = habl + ar   *Retroceder* = retroced + er
Cocinar = cocin + ar   *Exponer* = expon + er
Caminar = camin + ar   *Dormir* = dorm + ir
Correr = corr + er   *Requerir* = requer + ir

Depending or the last two letters of the verb, it will correspond to the first, second, or third conjugation.

Each of these conjugations has a different set of terminations to substitute those last two letters of the infinitive verb, keeping the root intact in each case.

Let's take a look at the following charts to see it more clearly.

Conjugation Of Regular Verbs Ending In -AR

Pronoun	HABLAR (To Speak)	COCINAR (To Cook)	CAMINAR (To Walk)
Yo (I)	Hablo (Speak)	Cocino (Cook)	Camino (Walk)
Tú (You)	Hablas (Speak)	Cocinas (Cook)	Caminas (Walk)
Vos (You)	Hablas (Speak)	Cocinas (Cook)	Caminas (Walk)
Usted (You)	Habla (Speak)	Cocina (Cook)	Camina (Walk)
Él/ Ella (He/She)	Habla (Speaks)	Cocina (Cooks)	Caminan (Walks)
Nosotros (We)	Hablamos (Speak)	Cocinamos (Cook)	Caminamos (Walk)
Vosotros (You)	Habláis (Speak)	Cocináis (Cook)	Camináis (Walk)
Ellos / Ellas (They)	Hablan (Speak)	Cocinan (Cook)	Caminan (Walk)

From this chart, we can understand several things:

- Every pronoun has its specific replacement for the termination −AR (-o, -as, -ás, -a, -a, -amos, -áis, -an).

- To conjugate a second person is a little trickier because it depends on the dialect you're using and if you're addressing a person formally of more familiarly, but as a general rule of thumb: For Tú, you change −AR by −AS; for Vos is almost the same, but you change the accent; for Usted, you change −AR by -A.

Conjugation Of Regular Verbs Ending In -ER

Pronoun	CORRER (To Run)	ENTENDER (To Understand)	DEFENDER (To Defend)
Yo (I)	Corro (Run)	Entiendo (Understand)	Defiendo (Defend)
Tú (You)	Corres (Run)	Entiendes (Understand)	Defiendes (Defend)
Vos (You)	Corres (Run)	Entiendes (Understand)	Defiendes (Defend)
Usted (You)	Corre (Run)	Entiende (Understand)	Defiende (Defend)
Él/ Ella (He/She)	Corre (Runs)	Entiende (Understands)	Defiende (Defends)
Nosotros (We)	Corremos (Run)	Entendemos (Understand)	Defendemos (Defend)
Vosotros (You)	Corréis (Run)	Entendéis (Understand)	Defendéis (Defend)
Ellos / Ellas (They)	Corren (Run)	Entienden (Understand)	Defienden (Defend)

- Every pronoun has its specific replacement for the termination –ER (-o, -es, -és, -e, -e, -emos, -éis, -en).
  - For Tú, you change –ER by –ES; for Vos is almost the same, but you change the accent; for Usted, you change –ER by –E.

Day 31. Conjugation Of Regular Verbs Ending In -IR

Pronoun	CONDUCIR (To Drive)	PERMITIR (To Allow)	RECIBIR (To Receive)
Yo (I)	Conduzco (Drive)	Permito (Allow)	Recibo (Receive)
Tú (You)	Conduces (Drive)	Permites (Allow)	Recibes (Receive)
Vos (You)	Conducís (Drive)	Permitís (Allow)	Recibís (Receive)
Usted (You)	Conduce (Drive)	Permite (Allow)	Recibe (Receive)
Él/ Ella (He/She)	Conduce (Drives)	Permite (Allows)	Recibe (Receives)
Nosotros (We)	Conducimos (Drive)	Permitimos (Allow)	Recibimos (Receive)
Vosotros (You)	Conducís (Drive)	Permitís (Allow)	Recibís (Receive)
Ellos / Ellas (They)	Conducen (Drive)	Permiten (Allow)	Reciben (Receive)

As in the first and second conjugations, for this third, there are several terminations each pronoun uses to substitute the termination -IR.

To conjugate a second person:

– For Tú, you change –IR by –ES

– For Vos you change –IR by –ÍS

- For Usted, you change –IR by -E

Some of the most commonly used regular verbs in Spanish are:

Alquilar	To Rent	Preguntar	To Ask (A Question)
Andar	To Walk	Regresar	To Return
Buscar	To Look For	Practicar	To Practice
Amar	To Love	Saludar	To Greet
Ayudar	To Help	Trabajar	To Work
Bailar	To Dance	Viajar	To Travel
Caminar	To Walk	Visitar	To Visit
Cantar	To Sing	Aprender	To Learn
Cocinar	To Cook	Beber	To Drink
Comprar	To Buy	Comer	To Eat
Contestar	To Answer	Correr	To Run
Dejar	To Leave	Creer	To Believe
Enseñar	To Teach	Leer	To Read
Desear	To Wish	Prometer	To Promise
Entrar	To Enter	Recorrer	To Go Over
Enviar	To Send	Romper	To Break
Escuchar	To Listen To	Temer	To Be Afraid
Esperar	To Wait	Vender	To Sell
Estudiar	To Study	Ver	To See
Firmar	To Sign	Abrir	To Open
Ganar	To Win	Admitir	To Admit
Gastar	To Spend	Aplaudir	To Clap
Hablar	To Speak	Asistir	To Assist
Lavar	To Wash	Describir	To Describe
Llevar	To Take	Escribir	To Write
Llegar	To Arrive	Percibir	To Perceive
Necesitar	To Need	Recibir	To Receive
Olvidar	To Forget	Subir	To Climb
Pagar	To Pay	Sufrir	To Suffer
Preparar	To Prepare	Vivir	To Live

Day 32. Irregular Verbs

Irregular verbs are those that don't follow the models explained above for the first, second, and third conjugations, but instead are conjugated in an entirely different and independent way.

These verbs are also different because, in some modes or tenses, they can modify the root word itself, something that never happens with regular verbs.

Types Of Irregular Verbs

This kind of verbs can be classified according to the way they modify the root word, in several categories:

Verbs With Vocalic Irregularities: The modification happens on some vowels, that can be joined in diphthongs or not. Examples:

- *Contar – Cuento*
  To Count – I Count

- *Fregar – Friego*

  To Scrub – I Scrub
- *Gobernar – Gobierno*

  To Govern – I Govern
- *Perder – Pierdo*

  To Lose – I Lose
- *Pensar – Pienso*

  To Think – I Think

Verbs With Consonantal Irregularities: This kind of verb adds one or more consonants into their conjugation, or substitute one consonant with another one. There are three terminations for this kind of verbs:

a. Termination *ecer*:

- *Atardecer – Llámame cuando al atardecer.*

  Sunset – Call me at sunset.
- *Enloquecer – Sabes que enloquezco con el azúcar.*

  Going crazy – You know I go crazy with sugar.

- *Enriquecer –Me gusta cuando enriquezco mi vocabulario.*

  Enrich – I like it when I enrich my vocabulary.

b. Termination *ducir*:

- *Traducir –Yo traduzco de Inglés a Español.*

  Translate – I translate from English into Spanish.

- *Introducir –Yo introduzco la clave.*

  Enter – I enter the password.

- *Deducir –No creo que ella deduzca eso.*

  Deduct – I don't think she will deduce that.

c. Termination *aer*:

- *Caer – No caigo en esos juegos.*

  Fall – I don`t fall in those traps.

- *Extraer –Extraigo la pulpa de la fruta.*

  Extract – I extract the pulp out of the fruit.

- *Traer – Traigo pizza para la cena.*

  Bring – I bring pizza for dinner.

Verbs With Mix Irregularities: These verbs modify both vowels and consonants of the root words.

- *Decir – Yo siempre te digo que hacer.*
  To tell – I always tell you what to do.

Verbs With Supplementary Roots: Verbs that can change their form completely because they come from two or more root words.

- *Ir – Iré a la playa mañana.*
  To go – I'll go to the beach tomorrow.
- *Ser – Somos los únicos hispanos acá.*
  To be – We´re the only Hispanics here.
- *Ser – Nosotros fuimos jefes de esa empresa.*
  To be –We were the bosses of that company.

Defective or Incomplete Verbs: These are verbs that don't have a complete conjugation because they're missing some modes or tenses, either because they refer to atmospheric phenomena or are not applicable to some situations.

Day 33. Social Situations

Enough theory for now!

It's time to get our learning motors running, so from now on, we will use the very basic foundations we have built for constructing short Spanish phrases that will be useful in several day-to-day situations.

Let's do it!

Greetings: Common Ways To Say Hi!

When you're meeting someone new, or when you see a person for the first time on the day, how to say hi is important to integrate and maybe can get you an interesting conversation.

- *Hola.*
  Hello.
- *Buenos días.*

Good morning.

- *Buenas tardes.*
  Good afternoon.
- *Buenas noches.*
  Good evening.
- *¿Cómo está?*
  How are you? (Formal)
- *¿Cómo estás?*
  How are you? (Informal)
- *¿Cómo están?*
  How are you? (Plural)
- *¿Qué tal?*
  How's it going?
- *¿Qué pasa?*
  What's happening? / What's up?
- *¿Qué hubo?*
  What happened?
- *Bienvenidos.*
  Welcome.
- *¿De dónde eres?*
  Where are you from?
- *¿Cómo te llamas?*

What's your name?

Day 34. Meet The Family

Hispanic culture gives the family a very high priority: the extended families are really important, and if you sometimes have the opportunity to attend a family party or just pay a visit to a Hispanic household, there are many typical phrases and expressions you may want to know in advance.

- *Él es mi tío Fernando.*
  He is my uncle Fernando.
- *Ella es mi prima, tiene 5 años.*
  She is my cousin, and she's five years old.
- *Mi hermano va a la universidad.*
  My brother goes to college.
- *Tengo una hermana menor.*
  I have a little sister.
- *Mi papá es genial.*
  My dad is great.
- *Amo a mi mamá.*
  I love my mom.
- *Saldré con mi tía.*

I will go out with my aunt.

- *Mi abuelo está viendo TV.*
  My grandpa is watching TV.

- *Mi hermana va a la escuela.*
  My sister goes to school.

- *Cocino con mi madre.*
  I cook with my mother.

- *Mi abuela cose.*
  My grandma sews.

- *Mi papá sabe conducir.*
  My dad knows how to drive.

- *¿Está tu padre en casa?*
  Is your father home?

- *Somos 4 hermanos.*
  We are 4 siblings.

- *Estamos en casa de mis padres.*
  We're at my parent's house.

- *Ana es mi suegra.*
  Ana is my mother in law.

Day 35. Going To School

There are many things to know about schools! Here are some phrases that can get you in context when going there.

- *La pizarra es verde.*
  The board is green.
- *A la hora del recreo.*
  During recess.
- *Los niños escriben.*
  The kids write.
- *Mi profesora es joven.*
  My teacher is young.
- *Mi amigo y yo estudiamos.*
  My friend and I study.
- *Uso mis colores.*
  I use my colors.
- *Me gustan las matemáticas.*
  I like mathematics.
- *Mi hermano está en primaria.*
  My brother is in elementary school.

- *El director es muy inteligente.*

  The principal is very intelligent.

- *Tengo muchos libros.*

  I have many books.

- *Me fue mal en el examen.*

  I didn't do well in the exam.

- *Cuento hasta cien.*

  I count to one hundred.

- *Mi escuela es blanca y verde.*

  My school is white and green.

- *Mi profesora explica muy bien.*

  My teacher explains very well.

- *Yo estudio química.*

  I study chemistry.

- *Voy en el bus escolar.*

  I'm going on the school bus.

- *Ella tiene un casillero.*

  She has a locker.

- *Juana está en el club de ajedrez.*

  Juana is in the chess club.

- *Tenemos un examen mañana.*

  We have a quiz tomorrow.

Day 36. Walking On The Street

Hispanic countries (almost in their entirety) have excellent weather all year round, and thus, people tend to be very active. Having some knowledge about street terms will come handy if you ever take a walk in Buenos Aires, Bogota, or Mexico City.

- *¿Cuál es la dirección de María?*
  What's Maria's address?
- *¿Cómo puedo llegar a la iglesia?*
  How do I get to church?
- *Calle 4, cruce con Avenida 1.*
  Street number 4 with Avenue 1.
- *José fue al centro.*
  José went downtown.
- *La plaza mayor.*
  Main Square.
- *Una cuadra.*
  A block.
- *El edificio alto a la derecha.*
  The high building at right.

- *Al doblar la esquina.*
  Around the corner.
- *La estación de policía.*
  The police station.
- *La estación de bomberos.*
  The fire station.
- *El chico pasea su perro.*
  The kid is walking his dog.
- *Esa es la panadería.*
  That is the bakery shop.
- *Manuel vio la farmacia.*
  Manuel saw the pharmacy.
- *La fuente está llena de gente.*
  The fountain is full of people.
- *El jardín de doña Josefa.*
  The garden of Ms. Josefa.
- *Cruza a la izquierda en el semáforo.*
  Turn left at the traffic light.

Day 37. A Visit To The Mall

Going shopping is so entertaining: you get to see what's new in the stores, buy those things you've always wanted and take advantage of the deals... *¿Cuánto cuesta eso?*

- *Vamos al centro comercial.*
  Let's go to the mall.
- *¿Tienen estacionamiento?*
  Do they have a parking lot?
- *En la tienda por departamentos.*
  On the department store.
- *¿Cómo puedo ayudarle?*
  How may I help you?
- *Quiero comprar un par de zapatos.*
  I want to buy a pair of shoes.
- *¿Cuánto cuestan?*
  How much do they cost?
- *¿Me los puedo probar?*
  Can I try them on?
- *Mi talla es 42.*

My size is 42.

- *¿Dónde puedo conseguir una camisa?*
  Where can I find a T-shirt?

- *¿Dónde consigo un pantalón?*
  Where can I find a pair of pants?

- *Me gustan esos jeans.*
  I like those jeans.

- *Vamos a comer helados.*
  Let's go eat some ice cream.

- *Hay una gran feria de comida.*
  There is a huge food court.

- *Aceptamos tarjetas de crédito.*
  We accept credit cards.

- *¿Tienes cambio?*
  Do you have change?

- *Solo efectivo.*
  Cash only.

- *La tienda está cerrada.*
  The store is closed.

- *La tienda está abierta.*
  The store is open.

Day 38. Let's Go To The Zoo

Exotic species from all around the world are gathered in this place: it makes it a perfect place to learn the Spanish names of the animals.

- *El gorila es grande.*
  The gorilla is big.
- *El león ruge.*
  The lion roars.
- *El pingüino es negro.*
  The penguin is black.
- *El pez nada.*
  The fish swims.
- *El tigre es naranja.*
  The tiger is orange.
- *El tiburón tiene muchos dientes.*
  The shark has a lot of teeth.
- *El canguro salta.*
  The kangaroo jumps.
- *La jirafa es alta.*
  The giraffe is tall.

- *La cebra tiene rayas.*
  The zebra has stripes.
- *El mono tiene cola.*
  The monkey has a tail.
- *El flamenco es rosa.*
  The flamingo is pink.
- *No alimentar a los animales.*
  Don't feed the animals.
- *Las serpientes son venenosas.*
  Snakes are venomous.
- *Los monos son divertidos.*
  The monkeys are funny.
- *No acaricie a los animales.*
  Don't pet the animals.
- *Zoológico de contacto.*
  Petting zoo.
- *El elefante es muy grande.*
  The elephant is very big.
- *El águila calva vuela alto.*
  The bald eagle flies high.
- *Juan es veterinario en el zoológico.*
  Juan is a vet at the zoo.

Day 39. A Tour On A University

Going to a university campus? Take notes on these phrases you'll definitely need to know.

- *¿Dónde está tu salón?*
  Where is your classroom?
- *¿A qué hora tienes clases?*
  At what time is your class?
- *Ahí viene el profesor de matemáticas.*
  There comes the math teacher.
- *Tengo examen más tarde.*
  I have a quiz later.
- *¿Qué idiomas estudias?*
  What languages do you study?
- *¿Tomas clases de francés?*
  Are you taking French classes?
- *¿Cómo te va con el inglés?*
  How are you doing with English?
- *Vas a ser abogado.*
  You're going to be a lawyer.
- *¿Te gusta la ingeniería?*

Do you like engineering?

- *¿Puedes prestarme tu lápiz?*
  Can you lend me your pencil?

- *¿Me prestarías tu bolígrafo?*
  Would you lend me your pen?

- *Tengo que estudiar esta noche.*
  I have to study tonight.

- *Mi cuaderno es azul.*
  My notebook is blue.

- *¿Dónde está mi libro de física?*
  Where is my physics book?

- *Esta es la facultad de medicina.*
  This is the Faculty of Medicine.

- *Departamento de investigación.*
  Research department.

- *Necesito ir al laborutorio.*
  I need to go to the lab.

- *Julio está en la biblioteca.*
  Julio is in the library.

- *Estoy en el primer semestre.*
  I'm in the first semester.

Day 40. A Walk On The Park

Vamos a dar un paseo en el parque. Do you want to know what things can be done in a park? Then keep on reading.

- *Mira, que lindos árboles hay aquí.*
  Look, there are very beautiful trees here.
- *Vamos por el camino de tierra.*
  Let's take the dirt track
- *Una ardilla está comiendo fruta en el suelo.*
  A squirrel is eating fruit on the floor.
- *¿Por qué hay tantas palomas acá?*
  Why are there so many doves in here?
- *Hay muchos niños jugando pelota.*
  There are many children playing with their balls.
- *¡Qué día tan bonito! El cielo está azul.*
  What a nice day! The sky is blue.

Day 41. What's In The Supermarket?

Meats, drinks, groceries, vegetables. So many things we all need; it's an absolute necessity to understand supermarket related phrases!

- *Tengo que ir al supermercado a comprar los víveres.*

  I have to go to the supermarket to buy groceries.

- *Necesito carne, pollo, pescado, vegetales, frutas.*

  I need meat, chicken, fish, vegetables, fruits.

- *Hay varios pasillos donde puede escoger las cosas que quiero.*

  There are several isles where I can choose the things I want.

- *Del pollo me gustan las alas, los muslos y la pechuga.*

  Of chicken, I like wings, thighs, and breast.

- *Compraré también varios tipos de pescado: sardinas, atún, salmón y pargo.*

I will also buy several types of fish: sardines, tuna, salmon, and snapper.

- *Frutas como el melón, la sandía, naranjas, bananas, piña, coco.*

  Fruits such as melon, watermelon, orange, banana, pineapple, coconut.

Day 42. Let's Go Dancing

Partying and dancing are a must if you go to a Spanish speaking country. You'll learn about the different music styles, where they're from, and maybe you'll want to learn how to move your body as a Latin lover.

- *¡Es hora de ir a la discoteca!*
  It's time to go to the disco!

- *Ahí podremos escuchar y bailar con muchos estilos de música.*
  There we can listen and dance many music styles.

- *La Salsa es un género muy popular, nacido de varios ritmos caribeños.*
  Salsa is a very popular genre, born from several Caribbean rhythms.

- *También podemos bailar merengue dominicano.*
  We can also dance Dominican merengue.

- *Desde hace algunos años, el reggaetón está de moda.*
  For some years, reggaeton is in fashion.

- *También puedes beber cerveza, whisky, un Cuba libre o quizás tequila.*

  You can also drink beer, whiskey, a Cuba libre, or maybe tequila.

Conclusion

As you can realize from a quick read of the book, learning Spanish is not so hard for English speakers as you might have thought. There are many similarities between these two languages that can and will facilitate the learning process for beginners. I hope you have found some valuable lessons in this book that will give you a head start on your journey.

My final recommendation would be to go out there and find someone to talk to. You can learn some things from this book as a start, but if you really want to master the language, interacting with others is a must: go to parties, talk to strangers on a bus, listen to music and speak with friends you know that speak the language.

Some other options are reading newspapers and magazines in Spanish, or maybe watching TV shows, movies from Latin America and / or Spain. Learning about the countries and their customs will also help you improve your vocabulary and give you many interesting topics to talk about. Going to Spanish-speaking countries as a tourist and trying to immerse yourself in the language is a wonderful way to learn the language as well, so if that's your goal, I would really recommend you to do it.

Disclaimer

The information contained in "**Daily Spanish For Beginners**" and its components, is meant to serve as a comprehensive collection of strategies that the author of this book has done research about. Summaries, strategies, tips, and tricks are only recommendations by the author, and reading this book will not guarantee that one's results will exactly mirror the author's results.

The author of this book has made all reasonable efforts to provide current and accurate information for the readers of this book. The author and its associates will not be held liable for any unintentional errors or omissions that may be found.

The material in the book may include information by third-parties. Third-party materials comprise of opinions expressed by their owners. As such, the author of this book does not assume responsibility or liability for any third-party material or opinions.

The publication of third-party material does not constitute the author's guarantee of any information, products, services, or opinions contained within third-party material. Use of third-party material does not guarantee that your results will mirror our results. Publication of such third-party material is simply a recommendation and expression of the author's own opinion of that material.

Whether because of the progression of the Internet, or the unforeseen changes in company policy and editorial submission guidelines, what is stated as fact at the time of this writing may become outdated or inapplicable later.

written expressed and signed permission from the author.